max fax

SHARKS

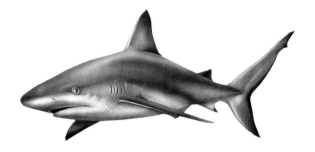

Max Fax:

SHARKS

Also in this series:
Space

Cover photograph: Sand Tiger Shark

Commissioning editor: Dereen Taylor
Series editor: Lisa Edwards
Book editor: Cath Senker
Designer: Luke Herriott
Language consultant: Wendy Cooling
Picture researcher: Shelley Noronha
Illustrator: Steve Roberts

Published in Great Britain in 2000
by Hodder Wayland, an imprint of
Hodder Children's Books
First published in paperback 2001

A Catalogue record for this book is available
from The British Library.

ISBN 0 7500 29722

Printed and bound in Italy by Eurografica S.p.a.

Hodder Children's Books
A division of Hodder Headline Ltd
338 Euston Road, London NW1 3BH

Note on sources: quotations on pages 11, 17 and 24 adapted
from *Sharks: Silent Hunters of the Deep* (Reader's Digest, 1986);
page 21 from *National Geographic* (January 1995).

SHARKS

Claire Llewellyn

HODDER
Wayland

an imprint of Hodder Children *'s Books*

CONTENTS

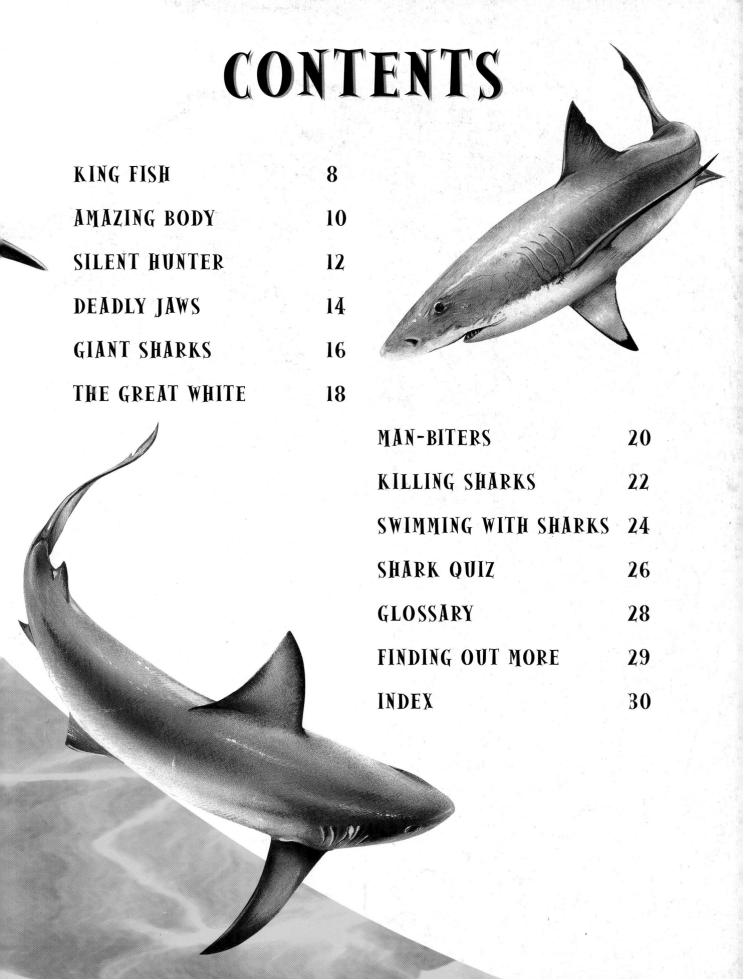

KING FISH

The shark is the king of the sea. It is fast and fierce. It fills people with fear. But that's not the whole story. Yes, some kinds of shark are dangerous, but most of them are harmless and shy.

The Caribbean Reef Shark – a 'typical' shark.

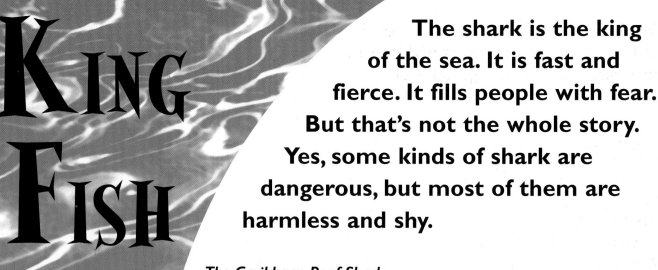

There are more than 350 kinds of shark in the sea, and they come in many shapes and sizes. The Pygmy Shark could lie in the palm of your hand. The Whale Shark is longer than a bus.

The Angel Shark is covered with spots and has a flat, rather flabby body. It buries itself in the sand on the sea-bed, and leaps out to catch its prey.

The Angel Shark.

The Sand Tiger Shark has long, ragged teeth, which give it a toothy grin. This shark looks very fierce but it is gentle with divers. It feeds on small fish and crabs.

The Sand Tiger Shark.

Have there always been sharks in the sea?

The first sharks were alive 370 million years ago – that's 200 million years before the first dinosaur.

How many are man-biters?

Nine: The Great White, Mako, Tiger, Bull, Great Hammerhead, Dusky, Oceanic White Tip, Blue and Lemon Shark.

Do all sharks live in the sea?

Most do – but the Bull Shark also swims in rivers.

The Spotted Wobbegong.

The Spotted Wobbegong lies like a rug on the sea-bed. The frills on its lips look like seaweed in the water. When small fish swim up to nibble them, the Wobbegong snaps them up!

AMAZING BODY

A shark's eye and skin.

Sharks spend their lives in water. They have the perfect body for the sea. It is smooth, strong and shaped like a torpedo. It is driven by a powerful tail.

A shark's eyes never close. When it is about to attack, a thin piece of skin slides over the eyes to give them extra protection.

The skin feels rough. It is covered with small, thorny scales called denticles.

A shark's teeth are triangular, and point backwards towards the throat. They have pointed tips and serrated edges, and cut just like a saw.

Gill slits
The gills take oxygen from the water, which then streams out through the gill slits.

Mouth
The mouth is tucked back under the snout. It takes in water as the shark swims along.

A shark's teeth.

Fins
The fins are like paddles. They keep the shark upright and help it to steer and turn in the water.

Skeleton
The skeleton is made of cartilage, not bone. Cartilage is light and rubbery.

DID YOU KNOW?

* Blue Sharks can easily swim over 3,500 km – that's the distance between London and Cairo.

* Sharks are so bendy that they can touch their tail with their nose.

* The Mako Shark can reach speeds of 50 kph – that's roughly as fast as a car.

Tail
The tail beats from side to side. This pushes the fish forwards.

Liver
The liver contains a lot of oil. Oil is lighter than water, and helps to keep the shark afloat.

SHARK ALERT
'I was snorkelling, gathering shells with two other divers... when I sensed something swimming very close to me. Thinking it was one of the other divers I looked around – straight into a large black eye. The fish flowed gently past, huge, beige-coloured, silent. I discovered that the shark was a female Tiger Shark, about 4.5 m long. She was probably simply passing by.'

Valerie Taylor, diver.

SILENT HUNTER

Sharks use their senses to find food in the water. They have good eyesight, sharp hearing, a keen sense of smell – and a few extra senses as well.

A head-on view of a Great Hammerhead Shark.

The Hammerhead Shark is a strange-looking fish, with a wide, flat, hammer-shaped head. The shark swings its head from side to side so that the eye and nostril on each end of the 'hammer' can pick up signals from the sea.

Ampullae of Lorenzini on a Blue Shark.

Sharks have electrical detectors on their snout. The tiny holes, known as ampullae of Lorenzini, pick up the weak electrical signals that every living thing gives out. This helps sharks to find their prey – even if it's hidden in the sand.

What do sharks eat?

Sharks eat almost anything – worms, fish, crabs, lobsters, turtles, penguins and seals. Some have even swallowed cans of paint!

Can sharks make a sound?

No. Sharks have no vocal cords inside their throat.

Do sharks have ears?

Yes. Their ears are inside their body, not on the outside like ours.

1. A shark picks up movements and the smell of blood.

2. It circles and 'bumps' its prey – a stingray.

3. Now the shark closes in for the kill.

Deadly Jaws

A shark's deadly jaws are lined with rows of sharp, jagged teeth. They crunch down on the prey.

Sharks are hunters. All hunters use weapons to kill their prey. Snakes have fangs. Eagles have claws. Sharks have massive jaws.

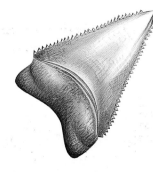

A shark's tooth is nearly as long as your thumb. This tooth is drawn lifesize.

Sharks lose a few teeth every time they attack. Rows of new teeth are always growing; they move forward to fill the gaps.

A Great White Shark lunges at a piece of tuna.

Sharks can bite, but they cannot chew. They shake their prey wildly and their jagged teeth 'saw' it into chunks.

Sharks torpedo towards their prey. They lift up their snout and lead with their jaws. The eyes roll back out of the way.

1. A shark attacks: the snout turns up...

DID YOU KNOW?

✳ Shark teeth are often washed up on the beaches of Florida, USA.

✳ A shark's tooth really is razor sharp. It could shave the hairs off your arm.

✳ Shark teeth slash and cut. They were once used on swords and knuckledusters.

2. the eyes roll back...

3. and the jaws thrust forward for the kill.

How big can a shark's mouth get?

An armchair would fit inside a Whale Shark's mouth. It's 1.2 m wide.

How many teeth does it have?

A shark has dozens of teeth, and gets through hundreds in its lifetime.

Can sharks taste their food?

Yes. They have taste buds on their tongue, around their mouth and even in their throat!

15

GIANT SHARKS

The Whale Shark is the biggest fish in the world. Yet, far from being dangerous, it's a gentle giant. It feeds on miniscule creatures, and will give people rides through the sea.

Whale Sharks can grow to over 18 metres – that's as long as eight divers swimming head to toe.

Whale Sharks feed on plankton – the tiny plants and animals that drift through the sea. To catch them, the sharks keep their mouths wide open. Masses of plankton float in through the jaws and are trapped in filters inside.

DID YOU KNOW?

* A Whale Shark swims at about 4 kph. That seems fast if you're riding on the tail.

* A Whale Shark's skin is 10 cm thick – thicker than any other animal's.

* Whale Sharks lay the world's largest eggs. They are roughly the size of a rugby ball.

This diver is swimming with a young Whale Shark off the coast of South America.

Divers sometimes swim with Whale Sharks. The fish allow people to grasp a fin and ride with them through the water.

Plankton is made up of masses of microscopic plants and animals. Together, they can weigh many tonnes.

Whale Sharks sometimes collide with boats. This is because the fish swim along very slowly, just below the surface of the sea. If the boat is small, it will probably be damaged. If it's big, the shark itself may die.

A Whale Shark swims along with its mouth wide open.

THE GREAT WHITE

A star in the cinema. A killer in the sea. The Great White is a large, fast, man-eating shark – it's the most dangerous fish in the sea.

How big is a Great White?

A Great White is 6 m long – about as long as two canoes. It weighs about 2 tonnes – that's as much as two cars.

How often does it need to eat?

After a big meal, a Great White can last 3 months before eating again.

What is the Great White's favourite food?

It loves seals and sea-lions.

Great Whites are the killers of the ocean. When they are hungry, they bite mouthfuls from whales. They swallow seals or sea-lions whole. They even bite human swimmers in two.

Great Whites are nosy animals. They are the only sharks to stick their heads out of the water. This can give fishermen a severe shock.

Great Whites are dark grey on top and white below. This is called countershading, and makes them very hard to see.

From below, it's hard to spot a shark against the light.

From above, it's hard to see a shark against the murky sea.

(Above) A Great White comes up to a diver in a cage.

(Right) Great Whites will attack boats until they sink. They may even try to leap aboard!

MAN-BITERS

Sharks kill 100 people every year. The hunters rarely eat their victims, so why do they attack? Are they defending their territory? Or is it just a terrible mistake?

Divers who swim in deep water are entering the world of the shark. Some sharks feel threatened by these intruders, and try to defend their 'space'. This may lead to a shark attack.

Sharks that feed on turtles and seals may attack people by mistake. From below, a surfer on a short surfboard looks just like a turtle. A diver looks like a seal.

DID YOU KNOW?

* Australia has recorded more shark attacks than any other country.

* Attacks are very rare. Even in Australia, you are 50 times more likely to drown than to be killed by a shark.

* A man is 13 times more likely than a woman to be attacked by a shark.

1. A swimmer on a surfboard...

2. looks like a turtle from below.

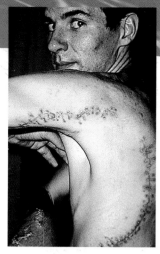
462 stitches, and lucky to be alive.

Not every shark attack ends in death. Some divers have remarkable escapes. But they carry scars for the rest of their life.

A Tiger Shark left its mark on this surfboard.

To reduce the risk of a shark attack:
• Never go in the sea if you are bleeding.
• Never swim alone after dark.
• Never swim where people are fishing.
• Never wear shiny jewellery in the water.
• Stay with other swimmers.
• If you see a shark, get out of the water as quickly and quietly as you can.

3. With a sickening jolt, the shark attacks. . .

4. and the dreadful jaws close on its 'prey'.

KILLING SHARKS

People kill sharks. We kill them for their meat, skin, teeth and oil. We kill them by accident. We kill them for sport. We kill about 100 million sharks every year.

How long do sharks live?

Many sharks live for 25 to 40 years. But Dogfish Sharks and Great Whites may live to be 100!

How do sharks die in the wild?

Small sharks are often eaten by larger sharks. Some die when they choke on their food. Others die of disease.

Who eats shark and chips?

British people love eating fish and chips. One fish they eat is the Dogfish Shark – usually called 'rock salmon'.

Some large sharks are now in danger, and may become extinct. Their numbers have fallen and might never recover. These sharks take many years to have young, and often have just one pup a year.

Many sharks die in meshing nets. These long nets are used to protect beaches from shark attack. Sharks that swim towards the beach get tangled in the nets and cannot escape. Most of them turn out to be harmless after all.

A Great White Shark, caught off the coast of Australia.

Giant sharks, such as the Great White, only exist in very small numbers. And yet fishermen try to catch them to win a prize. A shark's body is seen as a trophy. The jaws sell for thousands of pounds.

Most sharks are killed to make shark-fin soup. A shark's fins are sliced off and left to dry. The rest of its body is dumped in the sea.

(Above) A Grey Reef Shark, trapped in a meshing net.
(Right) Shark fins drying in the sun.

Swimming With Sharks

How do divers photograph sharks? They go to places where sharks are found and dive into the water. They take a bag of dead fish with them. Sharks nearby smell the blood. Minutes later, they suddenly appear.

A diver tests her chainmail suit. She has tempted a shark to bite her.

The metal suits worn by divers are made of thousands of tiny steel rings. These protect divers from a shark's sharp teeth.

SHARK ALERT

'My own experience with a White Tip happened while I was carrying out tests on a chainmail suit to see if it protected me against a shark attack. To tempt the shark to bite, I had to stuff fresh tuna pieces under the mesh, and wave a whole fish in front of it.'

Valerie Taylor, diver

Divers work inside a strong, steel cage when they photograph dangerous sharks. Excited sharks sometimes ram the cage but cannot get inside.

Filming sharks: these divers can close the cage the moment they feel in danger.

A diver in a shark scooter.

Divers ride in 'shark scooters' for extra protection. The scooters are made of strong, clear plastic and are powered by a small engine. They are a good way to explore a larger area.

DID YOU KNOW?

* Divers train sharks to swim to the sunny side of a boat to film them.

* The idea for chainmail diving suits came from the meat trade. Meat workers wear metal gloves to protect their hands from knives.

* To avoid attack, divers once tried wearing striped diving suits to look like poisonous stripy sea snakes.

SHARK QUIZ

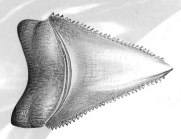

Can you find the right answers to these questions? They can all be found somewhere in this book. Check your answers on page 29.

1. How many kinds of shark are there?
a Nine
b About 100
c Over 350

2. Which of these sharks is harmless?
a The Whale Shark
b The Bull Shark
c The Mako Shark

3. What is a shark's skeleton made of?
a Rubber
b Bone
c Cartilage

4. Which part of a shark contains a lot of oil?
a Its skin
b Its liver
c Its fins

5. What is unusual about the Hammerhead Shark?
a It has a broad, flat head
b It has a very long tail
c It has just one eye

6. What are the ampullae of Lorenzini?
a Italian shark experts
b Small holes on a shark's snout that detect electrical signals
c Worms that live on the sea-bed

7. Why do sharks have so many teeth?
a To help them kill their prey
b To crush lobsters and crabs
c To replace ones that fall out

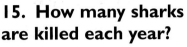

8. How do sharks cut up large prey?
a They shake it wildly
b They chew it into pieces
c They bang it against a rock

9. What do Whale Sharks eat?
a Whales
b Other sharks
c Plankton

10. Which shark is it possible to ride?
a The Great White Shark
b The Whale Shark
c The Spotted Wobbegong

11. How long is the Great White Shark?
a 2 metres
b 6 metres
c 18 metres

12. How many people die from shark attacks each year?
a About 10
b About 100
c About 1,000

13. Which country has the most shark attacks?
a Australia
b The USA
c South Africa

14. Which part of a shark is made into soup?
a Its eggs
b Its fins
c Its liver

15. How many sharks are killed each year?
a 1 million
b 10 million
c 100 million

16. How do divers attract sharks?
a By swimming at night
b By using dead fish as bait
c By splashing in the water

17. Where did the idea for chainmail diving suits come from?
a Workers in the meat trade
b Medieval knights
c Paris fashion designers

18. What is a shark scooter?
a A shark alarm
b A scooter for riding sharks
c A plastic underwater scooter

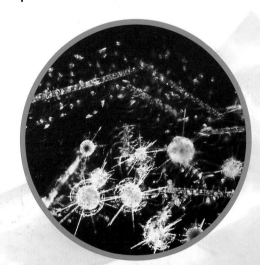

GLOSSARY

Cartilage The light, bendy material that makes up a shark's skeleton. You can feel a piece of cartilage at the end of your nose.

Chainmail A material made of small steel rings all linked together. Divers wear chainmail diving suits to protect themselves from sharks.

Countershading The name given to the shading on sharks and many other fish. A dark back and pale belly make fish harder to see.

Denticles The small, stiff, thorny scales that cover a shark's skin and protect it from being scratched.

Extinct Died out – no longer living in the world.

Gills The parts of a fish's body that allow it to breathe under water. The gills take in oxygen from the water and pass it on to the blood.

Microscopic Something so small that it can only be seen under a microscope.

Oxygen A gas that all animals need to breathe. Oxygen is one of the gases in air. It is also found in water.

Plankton Microscopic plants and animals that live in the sea. Several kinds of shark feed on plankton.

Prey Animals that are hunted by others for food.

Pup The name given to a baby shark.

Serrated Having a sharp, zig-zag edge like a steak knife or saw.

Shark-fin soup Soup made from shark fins, eaten mainly in the Far East, especially in Japan.

Skeleton The frame inside an animal's body that protects it and holds it up. In many animals the skeleton is made of bone. In sharks it is made of cartilage.

Taste buds Tiny cells inside an animal's mouth that help it to taste its food.

Territory A part of the sea where a shark hunts for food, and which it will defend against other sharks or divers.

Vocal cords Two strips of muscle inside the throat that allow us to speak and sing. Sharks do not have vocal cords.

FINDING OUT MORE

Books

Sharks: Silent Hunters of the Deep
(Reader's Digest, 1986)

I didn't Know that Sharks keep Losing their Teeth and other Amazing Facts about Sharks by Claire Llewellyn (Aladdin/Watts, 1998)

Eyewitness Shark by Miranda MacQuitty (Dorling Kindersley, 1992)

Sharks by M. Oakley (Ladybird, 1995)

Sharks by Doug Perrine (Colin Baxter Photography Ltd, 1995)

Sharks by Seymour Simon (HarperCollins, 1995)

Sharks by Erik D. Stoops & Sherrie Stoops (Sterling Publishing Co. Inc., 1994)

Sharks by Niki Walker and Bobbie Kalman (Crabtree, 1997)

Videos

Shark (a BBC programme produced on video by Dorling Kindersley)

Websites

http://ds.dial.pipex.com/sharktrust/info/shtml
www.aquanet.com
www.greenmarine.com
www.oceanstar.com/shark

Places to visit

You can see sharks at aquaria and sea-life centres in the following towns: Birmingham, Blackpool, Bray, Brighton, Great Yarmouth, Hastings, Hunstanton, Newquay, Oban, Plymouth, Portsmouth, Rhyl, St Andrews, Scarborough, Southend-on-Sea, Tynemouth, Weston-Super-Mare and Weymouth.

Answers to quiz

1	c	7	c	13	a
2	a	8	a	14	b
3	c	9	c	15	c
4	b	10	b	16	b
5	a	11	b	17	a
6	b	12	b	18	c

INDEX

Page numbers in **bold** mean there is a picture on the page.

Picture acknowledgements

Ardea (Ian Gordon) 9 (below), (Ron and Valerie Taylor) 12, (V. Taylor) 13, (V. Taylor) 19, (R. and V. Taylor) 21 (above), (Adrian Warren) 21 (below), (V. Taylor) 23 (above), (R. and V. Taylor) 24; Bruce Coleman *Cover*; (Franco Banfi) 16; Getty Images (Stuart Westmorland) 8 (above), (Jeff Rotman) 14, (Jeff Rotman) 18, (Fred Bavendam) 22, (Andrew Drake) 25; Natural History Picture Agency (Norbert Wu) 9 (above), (G. I. Bernard) 10 (above), (Norbert Wu) 10 (below), 17; Oxford Scientific Films (Norbert Wu) 8 (below), (Aloo Brando) 16–17 (main picture); Planet Earth Pictures (Alex Kerstitch) 23 (below).